I Love You Because...

A Keepsake Journal of Our Love

Fill-in-the-blanks and share!

Published by Neuron Publishing
www.LoveBookOnline.com

Write your own love story...

♡

Share and express your love by saying exactly WHY you love your partner. This beautifully illustrated book will guide you through all the joys and fun of your relationship by answering the questions and filling in the blanks. It's a true exploration of your relationship and what you and your partner contribute to the relationship. It's fun, light hearted and the perfect romantic gift to explore the true reasons why you love each other.

"Grow old along with me!
The best is yet to be..."

- Robert Browning

This book is dedicated to

_____

with love, from

_____

Our relationship

It was love at
first glance.

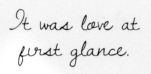

I love you because...

our story began...

_____

_____

_____

_____

one of my first thoughts about you was...

_____

_____

right off the bat, I liked that you...

_____

_____

My love for
you grows more
each day.

8

I love you because...

you take responsibility for...

_____

_____

_____

_____

this helps our relationship because...

_____

_____

I don't have to worry about...

_____

_____

We balance each other well.

I love you because...

we agree on...

_____

_____

_____

_____

but we agree to disagree on...

_____

_____

we balance each other by...

_____

_____

You are my rock.

trust

Compassion

love

faith

values

appreciation

respect

honesty

humor

admiration

loyalty

communication

assion

equality

12

romance

patien

I love you because...

our relationship is built on...

_____

_____

_____

_____

we've created a strong bond by...

_____

_____

we can make our future even better by...

_____

_____

I'm glad you let me
into your heart.

I love you because...

only I know...

_____

_____

_____

_____ about you.

and only you know...

_____

_____ about me.

trusting each other means...

_____

_____

You're my best friend.

I love you because...

one thing that brought us closer together was...

_____

_____

_____

_____

afterwards, I remember thinking...

_____

_____

it was a turning point because...

_____

_____

I love you because...

our best bonding time is...

_____

_____

_____

_____

we show affection by...

_____

_____

_____

_____

our terms of endearment include...

_____

_____

_____

_____

we communicate mostly by...

_____

_____

_____

_____

I'll share all my
dreams with you.

I love you because...

we dream about our future together, such as...

_____

_____

_____

_____

we can make them a reality by...

_____

_____

I'm most excited about...

_____

_____

Love is the fabric
that holds us together.

I love you because...

I knew I was in love when...

_____

_____

_____

_____

what I remember most about that time is...

_____

_____

I realized you loved me when...

_____

_____

Let's grow
old together

24

I love you because...

our relationship has grown by...

_____

_____

_____

_____

you've helped make that happen by...

_____

_____

we can continue to grow together by...

_____

_____

About you

Life is delectable
with you in it.

I love you because...

your favorite types of foods are...

_____

_____

_____

_____

your preferred place/way to eat it is...

_____

_____

I realized you loved it when...

_____

_____

Spoiler alert:
we have a
happy ending!

I love you because...

your favorite types of movies are...

_____

_____

_____

_____

your thoughts on them are...

_____

_____

we can always agree on watching...

_____

_____

I love getting
lost with you.

I love you because...

your favorite thing to do on a lazy day is...

_____

_____

_____

_____

_____

my favorite lazy day memory with you is...

_____

_____

_____

_____

I have the most
fun with you!

I love you because...

you have fun doing...

_____

_____

_____

_____

one of the best times we've had together was...

_____

_____

I really enjoy doing...

_____

_____ with you.

No day is boring
when you're around.

I love you because...

your favorite pastime is...

_____

_____

_____

_____

my favorite memory of us doing it is...

_____

_____

you've encouraged me to try...

_____

_____

I love you because...

your biggest pet peeve is...

_____

_____

_____

_____

your biggest life achievement is...

_____

_____

_____

_____

your greatest addiction is...

_____

_____

_____

_____

you love...

_____

_____

_____

_____

*Life is sweeter
with you in it.*

I love you because...

you like to indulge by...

_____

_____

_____

_____

and that you like to do it while...

_____

_____

I like to spoil you by...

_____

_____

I'll accept you no
matter what.

I love you because...

your guilty pleasure is...

_____

_____

_____

_____

I like to share in...

_____

_____ with you.

I pretend not to notice...

_____

_____

You're the greatest
nurturer I know.

I love you because...

you care about...

_____

_____

_____

_____

your passion about it makes me feel...

_____

_____

I love how important...

_____

_____ is to you.

I love how you
speak your mind.

I love you because...

you have strong views & opinions on...

_____

_____

_____

_____

you respect my thoughts on...

_____

_____

I love to hear your opinions about...

_____

_____

Things you do for me

You've never let
me down.

I love you because...

you supported me when...

_____

_____

_____

_____

if they gave awards for support, you'd receive...

_____

_____

I can't imagine going through...

_____

_____ without you.

You always point me in the right direction.

I love you because...

you give great advice, the best being...

_____

_____

_____

_____

a specific time you helped me was when...

_____

_____

you've helped me think differently
about things, such as...

_____

_____

You always know
how to make
me smile.

I love you because...

you can always surprise me by...

_____

_____

_____

_____

the best surprise you've given me was...

_____

_____

your thoughtfulness makes me feel...

_____

_____

You know what really gets me!

HA HA HA HA HA HA!

I love you because...

you can always make me laugh by...

_____

_____

_____

_____

the funniest thing you've ever done is...

_____

_____

_____

I'd describe your sense of humor as...

_____

I'm never in need when I have you.

I love you because...

you share your...

_____

_____

_____

_____ with me.

the most meaningful things we've shared are...

_____

_____

_____

_____

_____

_____

I love you because...

you've made sacrifices for me by...

_____

_____

_____

_____

the best gift you've given me was...

_____

_____

_____

_____

you cheer me up when...

_____

_____

_____

_____

you always know what I need, like...

_____

_____

_____

_____

Just keep
swimming.

I love you because...

you encouraged me when...

_____
_____
_____
_____

your support made me feel...

_____
_____

you motivate me most when you...

_____
_____

You've taught me
so much.

I love you because...

you've taught me...

_____

_____

_____

_____

and it's made me a better person by...

_____

_____

together, we've learned how to...

_____

_____

Your kind soul
has opened my
heart.

I love you because...

you've changed my world for the better by...

_____

_____

_____

_____

the biggest impact you've had on me is...

_____

_____

without you, my life would be...

_____

_____

Your love means everything to me.

I love you because...

you make me feel loved when you...

_____

_____

_____

_____

I receive your love best when...

_____

_____

we prefer to show love by...

_____

_____

I still get
butterflies when
you're around.

I love you because...

you excite me when you...

_____

_____

_____

_____

and I excite you by...

_____

_____

I can't get enough when you...

_____

_____

Things we do together

We make the best team.

I love you because...

we work together on...

_____

_____

_____

_____

my favorite project we've done together was...

_____

_____

we're a great team when we...

_____

_____

I'll go anywhere
with you.

I love you because...

we've travelled to...

_____

_____

_____

_____

and that we also want to go to...

_____

_____

my favorite vacation was...

_____

_____

I'm always on the
right path with you.

I love you because...

we plan things together, like...

_____

_____

_____

_____

I love looking forward to...

_____

_____

_____

_____

_____

_____ with you.

The stars aligned
when I met you.

I love you because...

we are so compatible...

_____
_____
_____
_____

because...

_____
_____

we could be even better by...

_____
_____

I only want to be with you.

I love you because...

your kisses are...

_____

_____

_____

_____

the best kiss we've had is...

_____

_____

our first kiss was...

_____

_____

I love you because...

my favorite part of our daily routine is...

_____

_____

_____

_____

our favorite restaurant is...

_____

_____

_____

_____

our favorite way to let loose is...

_____

_____

_____

_____

our most romantic moment was...

_____

_____

_____

_____

I love that we're
young at heart.

I love you because...

one of the goofiest things we've done is...

_____
_____
_____
_____

I love it because...

_____
_____

The last time we laughed that hard was...

_____
_____

Adventure awaits!

I love you because...

we have fun adventures, like...

_____

_____

_____

_____

what I remember most about them is...

_____

_____

we should have more adventures, like...

_____

_____

Every day is
merry with you.

I love you because...

we spend the holidays together, like...

_____

_____

_____

_____

my favorite memory is...

_____

_____

we have (or can make) holiday traditions, such as...

_____

_____

We can make it
through anything!

I love you because...

together, we have overcome...

_____

_____

_____

_____

the key to our success was...

_____

_____

getting through it made me feel...

_____

_____

Qualities

You never cease
to amaze me!

I love you because...

your best talent is...

_____

_____

_____

_____

you worked so hard to...

_____

_____

I admire this because...

_____

_____

Your smile can change
my entire day.

I love you because...

you bring out the best in me, specifically...

_____

_____

_____

_____

and you compliment me by...

_____

_____

we're unstoppable when it comes to...

_____

_____

You are so
dear to me.

I love you because...

a quality I admire about you is...

_____

_____

_____

_____

it has taught me...

_____

_____

I wish I was more...

_____

_____, like you.

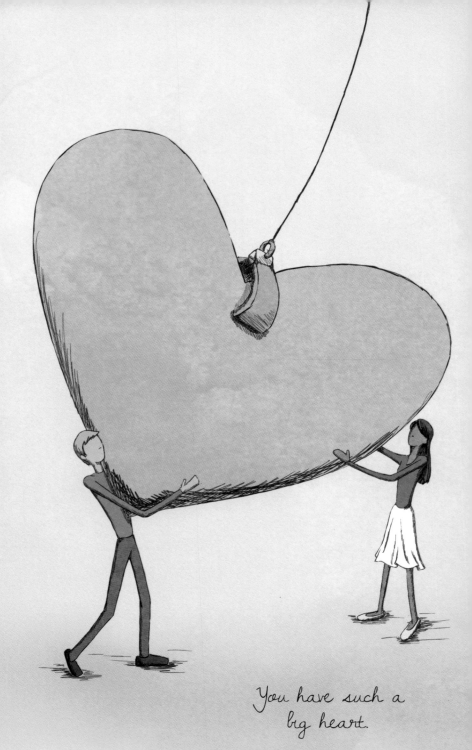

You have such a
big heart.

I love you because...

you show kindness by...

_____

_____

_____

_____

your kind heart makes me feel...

_____

_____

I am so grateful when you...

_____

_____

I'd steal the
moon and stars
for you.

I love you because...

the most endearing thing about you is...

_____

_____

_____

_____

because...

_____

_____

my favorite memory of your cuteness is...

_____

_____

You've made me
a better person.

I love you because...

your core values are...

_____

_____

_____

_____

and that we share these values...

_____

_____

If we have children, we want to raise them to...

_____

_____

I love you because...

my favorite physical feature of yours is...

_____

_____

_____

_____

you can really appreciate...

_____

_____

_____

_____

people would describe your personality as...

_____

_____

_____

_____

you are knowledgeable in the area of...

_____

_____

_____

_____

Your strength
astounds me.

I love you because...

your greatest strength is...

_____

_____

_____

_____

you show how strong you are when...

_____

_____

I admire that you are able to...

_____

_____

I love you because...

you are not afraid of...

_____

_____

_____

_____

a fear we've faced together is...

_____

_____

you are open with me about your fear of...

_____

_____

You always
have a positive
outlook on life.

I love you because...

you are open-minded about...

_____

_____

_____

_____

you inspire me to...

_____

_____

you're willing to try...

_____

_____

I will love you
forever.

I love you because...

you just simply are...

_____

_____

_____

_____

to me, you are...

_____

_____

to others, you are...

_____

_____

About LoveBook

We are a group of individuals who want to
spread love in all its forms. We believe love fuels
the world and every relationship is important. We
hope this book helps build on that belief.